A Graduate's Guide to Life

A GRADUATE'S GUIDE TO LIFE

Three Things They Don't Teach You in College
That Could Make All the Difference

FRANK J. HANNA

BEACON PUBLISHING
North Palm Beach, Florida

Design by Ashley Wirfel

ISBN: 978-1-929266-27-2 (hardcover)

Beacon Publishing, Inc.
631 US Highway 1, Suite 403
North Palm Beach, FL 33408

Second printing, April 2018

Printed in the United States of America

INTRODUCTION

Within the pages of this short book, I'm going to give you a recipe for becoming successful. This recipe only has three ingredients: an understanding of **reality**, an understanding of **competition**, and an understanding of **wealth**. These concepts are not complex, so it won't take us long. You'll see.

I've gone through a lot of formal schooling, worked at a major law firm, started several businesses, taken a company public, and worked with leaders as diverse as the president and the pope. And I discovered that, oddly enough, these three ingredients for success are not only not taught in college—they're not really taught anywhere! Those who are happy in life usually stumble upon them eventually, but many folks never learn about them, and many learn them too late. I believe the sooner you know them, and live them, the happier you will be.

So first, a question: How many of you and your friends were told as you headed off to college that these would be the best four years of your life?

By the way, this is a rhetorical question. In other words, I already know the answer, because I have asked numerous groups of college students this question. The answer is: all of you. All of you were told, by someone, perhaps your parents, that your college years should be the best four years of your life. But you know what? It is *horrible* advice! Truly terrible. It can send you down the wrong path and have negative consequences in your life.

In the following chapters, I'll show you why and give you a better alternative. Let's start by taking a look at the first ingredient in the wealth recipe: an understanding of reality.

An Understanding
of Reality

Seriously, do you really want to think that your college years are the best years of your life, and the rest of life is all downhill? How does that make you feel? What a ridiculous strategy for life!

Why do people say this? Well, there are a variety of reasons that we won't go into in this particular book. Interestingly enough, the folks who tell you this may include your parents and other adults who care deeply for you. Suffice it to say, when folks say this, they are not thinking clearly about human nature and happiness.

All you have to do is ask yourself, "Do I hope that my college years are the best years I will ever have, never to be matched again for the next seventy years I live? Or, while college might be a wonderful experience, am I actually hopeful that life will continue to get better—and happier?"

Aren't those two questions remarkably easy to answer? Of course you don't want college to be the best years of your entire life. Of course you hope that life will continue to get better after college. I am much happier now than I was in college. And I know many, many others who can say the same thing. So let's figure out how you can be one of them.

But in order to do that, we will have to examine reality—the way things really are. Because often the world tells you stupid things (like college should be the best time of your life). College should be great, but don't set that low of a bar for the rest of your life. Don't put that kind of limitation on your happiness.

So—are you willing to look at things as they truly are? Because it's pretty hard to do. On the other hand, who wants to be delusional? I doubt you are saying, "I want to be delusional—I would rather not see things as they really are."

My favorite definition of education is from Josef Jungmann. He said that "education is the process of introducing a person to reality." I love that definition, and it is so true. I have been involved with the field of education for many years, and I have helped to start a number of educational institutions, and I know from firsthand experience that this is indeed the goal of education—to introduce a person to *reality*.

However, sometimes reality is a hard thing. Reality can be painful. There is a reason people don't go to the doctor when something is wrong; they don't want to hear the diagnosis. They would rather delude themselves than face the reality that something might be wrong.

The great poet T. S. Eliot captured this phenomenon precisely when he said in his famous poem "Burnt Norton," the first poem in his collection *Four Quartets*, that "humankind cannot bear very much reality." He knew! He knew that we avoid reality.

I see this phenomenon all the time in the business and investment world. People love to fool themselves, to provide an answer that is more palatable, even if it is wrong. It is so prevalent that, in order to guard against it, we developed a concept in our business called "reality-based management." In other words, manage based on the way things actually are, rather than how you wish they were. We even created a slogan for our business: "Measured by reality."

Therefore, if you want to be wealthy, you are going to have to ask yourself, "Am I willing to deal with reality? Do I have the courage and fortitude to see things as they really are?"

Stated another way, can you ask "Why?" and keep on asking "Why?" If you can—and I *strongly* suggest that you try—you have a good chance of being wealthy.

You see, I want to change how you think about your future.

An Understanding
of Competition

Now let's look at the topic of how we get ahead. That's the phrase we use when we are thinking about being successful, isn't it? *Get ahead.* This is another one of those things people who care for us tell us we should do.

But have you ever really thought about that phrase? You know it is a distinctly competitive phrase. In order to "get ahead," we presumably must "get ahead" of *someone.* In its essence, "getting ahead" is a competitive enterprise. I learned this the hard way, and it almost led to financial ruin.

My brother and I had a thriving business. Only ten years after opening its doors, we had four million customers. In that industry, there were four other companies with whom we were competing for the same customers.

In 2007 we began seeing warning signs of an economic downturn. We were nervous, and because we were concerned that the price of the inventory we would have to buy to sell to our customers might start climbing, we dramatically slowed down our marketing efforts. We subsequently lost a lot of our customers, and we have not been able to regain them.

Today we have less than one million customers. Our stock price in 2007 was $40 per share, and by 2016, on an adjusted basis, it was around $15.

What might my brother and I have done differently in order to have competed more success-fully?

Looking at the facts, the scenario plays out like a real failure. And in absolute numbers, it is. Howev-er, there is more to the story. It gets a bit more inter-esting when other facts come to light. For example, of the four competitors (who, by the way, sold more and more product as we reduced our marketing efforts), three of them went bankrupt and no longer even exist. The final competitor avoided bankruptcy only by being bailed out by the government. In other words, its business was effectively bankrupted, too.

The point is that by deciding not to compete in 2007, we kept our company alive. While it's now worth less than half of what it was, it still has a lot of value, and we did not go bankrupt. We survived by withdrawing from the competition.

We live in America, where competition is seen as an unalloyed good. But is it? Remember, part of our challenge when looking at reality is to keep asking "Why?" So let's continue to ask some tough questions, all of which relate to "getting ahead" and managing the risks of that endeavor.

First, though, let's look at another case. Imagine you are back in high school, and you are at a basketball game. Your team is playing the crosstown rival. For the last ten years, this team has won the city championship. Now, for the first time ever, *your* team has a chance to win.

The final buzzer sounds, and your team appears to have won by one point! However, you suddenly notice that as the game ended, the other team was shooting, and a foul was called.

The player for the other team goes to the foul line for two shots. He makes the first shot, tying the game. Now he is shooting the final shot. If he misses, the game will go to overtime, and your team still has a chance to win. If he makes it, your rival wins the city championship once again.

Do you yell and hope that he misses, or do you hope that he makes the foul shot?

This is another one of those rhetorical questions, or at least semi-rhetorical. I have asked this question many, many times, and I always get the same response. Everyone hopes he misses.

And then I ask another question. "What is the purpose of competition?" And the answer is always, "To win!" In fact, this answer comes out so quickly, so reflexively, it almost seems to be instinctive. And in fact, biologically, it is instinctive. But it is not the correct answer. It is not the answer that leads to success and happiness.

Let me break that down just a bit. Our desire to compete *is* biological. Watch any nature show, and within ten minutes you will see the animals competing. They compete for food, water, power, respect, and sex. Those who win the competition survive, and those who lose often die.

While we human beings are indeed animals, and we also need food, water, power, respect, and sex, we are MORE than animals. And so, over time, in civilization (the very word means not acting like animals), we have learned how to make this process of competing less animal, and more human. And amazingly enough, we have figured out how to get wealthy *without* competing!

Regardless of your religious or ethical beliefs, most scientists concur that over the past ten thousand years human beings have built increasingly sophisticated and prosperous civilizations via cooperation, not competition.

Here's another question. Do you believe that for a human being to be happy, he or she should be more like a human, or more like an animal? Have you ever watched an eagle soar, or a cheetah run, or a dolphin swim? There is an incredible beauty in seeing those creatures do what they were intended to do. It is actually inspirational—when we see it, spirit is breathed into us.

That is what it is like for a human being to be fully human, not just an animal. It is inspirational when a human being is noble and heroic. It is life-giving.

Therefore, the correct answer, when the other team's player is at the foul line at the end of the game, is that you should hope he or she makes the shot.

When you think about it, of course that is the right answer! Why, as a human being, should you ever wish ill on someone else who has done nothing wrong? There is nothing noble, heroic, or in the end, human, about that. That kind of wish is the animal inside of us.

THE REAL PURPOSE OF HUMAN COMPETITION

You see, the purpose of *human* competition, as opposed to *animal* competition, is to become more fully human! It's in bringing out the hero in ourselves, and in those with whom we are competing. The competition has been a success if it accomplishes this, and if it does not, it is not a success, no matter who wins or loses.

There is much about Tiger Woods' behavior that I do not admire, but a comment he made years ago helped me realize this phenomenon about competition. Tiger was competing in a major championship, and he ended the tournament tied for the lead, which meant going to a playoff. In the playoff, there was a hole where Tiger had made his putt, and his opponent had a thirty-foot putt to tie the game and keep the tournament going.

After the tournament, a reporter asked Tiger, "What were you thinking about while your opponent was standing over his putt?"

Tiger responded, "I was hoping he would make it."

The reporter responded, "Really?"

Tiger said, "Yes—when you are competing, you want the other person to play at his best. That's what it is all about."

As a human being, we should never, ever find ourselves wishing misfortune or failure on another human being. It detracts from our own dignity and humanity.

The human way to compete, as opposed to the animal way, is with love and prudence.

Love and prudence? Those are the essential components of competition? And the answer is yes. Love, so you may enhance your integrity as a human being, and prudence, to tell you when to pull out of a destructive competition.

Regarding love, we will content ourselves with a simple definition for now: Love is the action of sacrificing for the good of another. If you can compete with love—that is, wishing the best for your competitor, then competition can make you more human . . . and more successful. This is what *amateur* sports were all about, and it's the reason the Olympics were limited to amateurs for so long. The root word of *amateur*, *amat*, means "to love." Good sportsmanship is an outgrowth of this philosophy of competition.

Good competition, with love, can raise us to heroic heights. We find ourselves pushing with more energy and force than we might have thought possible. But we should also hope that our competitors can do the same thing—push themselves past where they thought possible, into the realm of the heroic. It is only human competition when both of these elements exist; otherwise, it is the activity of mere animals.

Unfortunately, when competition is missing love, it becomes more like war, as can be seen in the language surrounding so many of our sporting events today. And who wants to be at war all the time, or thinks that being at war makes one happy or successful?

How Competition Can Destroy Success

I believe a proper understanding of the ethics of competition and "getting ahead" are critical in our eventual understanding of how to be successful.

So here is the *key point* about competition and becoming successful: *Competition is not necessary for you to be successful.* You don't have to compete for success, and many times, competition will destroy your happiness. Competition is an inevitable part of our animal world, but it is very hazardous for success creation. It actually led to the very first murder in history, when Cain killed his brother, Abel.

The world tells you that the way to be successful is to get ahead, to beat others, and that to do this, you have to compete; you have to win at all costs. But I am going to show you how to become successful without getting caught up in this nonsense.

I know this viewpoint may be exceedingly contrary to your current thinking. So before diving into it further, let me tell you—as someone who has been deeply involved in the financial world for the last twenty-five years—how competition *destroyed a huge portion of the world's wealth* during the great global economic crisis of 2008–09. Let me tell you how the world economy was brought to its knees, businesses were destroyed, and countries were bankrupted, all because of the inability to walk away from the competition.

When folks comment on the global financial meltdown of 2008–09, it is very easy for them to say that people should have known better than to take on as much debt as they did, so as not to jeopardize their very survival. But that is easier said than done. When Charles Prince, the former CEO of Citicorp, was asked why his bank continued to take on increasing amounts of risk, he replied, "When the music plays, you dance."

This quote has been used as a means of expressing disdain for Wall Street, but all Prince was doing was telling the truth. What he meant was that, in a competitive system, if you don't keep up with what those around you are doing in the game, you will lose.

You're left with three options: violate your conscience and have a chance to win, follow your conscience and probably lose, or stop playing the game. Our pride usually keeps us from quitting the game. I mean, who wants to be a quitter? And so Charles Prince, and others in his industry, kept taking on more and more risk, even though they knew it was hazardous.

And by the way, this dance does not just happen in banking and financial circles. It happens in other businesses, too. Any time a competitor of yours gains an advantage through taking extra risk, there is always the temptation to do the same. I invest in private equity and venture capital, which means that I have looked at and reviewed hundreds of businesses, and I have seen this temptation in every one of them.

It doesn't just happen in business; it happens in sports. A few years ago I read about a man who was drafted to play pro baseball. He was selected before Derek Jeter. For those of you who don't know, Derek Jeter played for the New York Yankees, and is one of the best players in the last twenty-five years of baseball. But this player, who was projected to be even better than Derek Jeter, did not make it in the major leagues. Later, when asked about not making it to the majors, and whether he wished he had used steroid drugs, he said, "Yes, if I had used them, I think I could have had a successful career, and so many other players were using them." Note: Steroids can destroy one's health and are against the rules, but this player regrets not taking them.

But it's not just in sports. The competition to get into good colleges is so intense that high school students are taking Ritalin to enhance their concentration when taking the SAT and ACT. This medication is often obtained with the consent of their parents, with a doctor's prescription for attention deficit disorder. And in college, there is a black market for these same drugs right before exam time.

Even worse, many of the mothers of these kids, who want to impress all the other mothers with their ability to be a Super Mom, steal the Ritalin from their children to boost their own energy and concentration. For that matter, it is reported that a surprising number of all breast enhancement surgeries are second surgeries designed to make them even bigger. These are the same mothers who, along with their husbands, send their children to three different summer camps to train in certain athletic endeavors in order to gain an advantage against the other children.

The debt, the excess risk, the steroids, the Ritalin are all forms of imprudent risk—i.e., a way to get more return by taking on too much risk. And the reason we do it is pride. We don't want to lose. And because no one tells us that pride is a sin, we think of it as a virtue, and we believe that whatever we do out of our sense of pride is OK. The problem is, pride won't make you successful. It only makes you anxious and desperate.

So while we rail against greed, pretending that if we could just take care of the greed of the 1 percent of the population who exploits the rest of us, things would be fine, we simultaneously ignore the real sins that pervade our societies at every level. The real and present issue, for all of us, is when to pull out of the competition rather than forfeit our integrity, and our humanity.

And that determination requires prudence.

Prudence, briefly stated, is the use of wisdom to act in the right manner in the circumstances in which we find ourselves. Prudence is what helps us determine when to pull out of the competition, rather than jeopardize our integrity and humanity. Prudence is what helps us weigh the costs and benefits of competing in a particular area. It is the conscious development and commitment to a prudent review of our circumstances that can help overcome the pride that keeps us dancing to the music, even when it is about to kill us.

Abundance and Value—an Alternative Way

You might be thinking, *If I don't compete, and compete well, how will I ever succeed, prosper, or be wealthy?* But if you are asking this question, it's because you have been told that to succeed, you must get ahead, and getting ahead means getting ahead of others, and getting ahead of others means beating them. You know—the early bird gets the worm! Well, I don't want a worm, and I don't like getting up early. So let's see if we can think through a different paradigm (which is a system of thinking) for succeeding.

You see, I don't want most of my life filled with competition. If I want to be happy, I want it filled with *abundance*. This is the new paradigm for wealth. I don't want to win a competition—I want a shower of blessings—a shower of good things.

Isn't that what you would want for your children? What parents want their own children to constantly compete against one another? What parents want their children to be rivals? No! Parents want their children to be filled with abundant blessings. The question is not which child "gets ahead." The question is how all their children can be happy!

For myself, I don't want any rivals. Why would I want a rival? Why would I want to have someone who *wants me to lose?* But if I don't want rivals, I can't be one myself.

My brother and I have now been working together for twenty-five years. For the first twenty-five years of our lives, we competed all the time. For the second twenty-five years, how often do you think we have competed? Hardly ever. It is not good for us. I am not interested in getting ahead of him, and he is not interested in getting ahead of me.

I don't want to compete with my wife. I don't want to compete with her for our child's affection, and I don't want to compete with other men for her affection. The whole competition thing is so vastly overrated, and its danger is so vastly understated.

But if I am prudent—if I have my eyes wide open to reality—I can focus on that which can truly make me happy. Let's face it—most of us would say that *wealth is having an abundance of that which we value.*

Our education system does not prepare us for this kind of thinking. Instead, everything in our education system is based on rankings and competition. For that matter, most of our common culture is based on rankings and competition. How many Top Ten lists do we run across almost every day?

Internet analytics have proven to advertisers that more people will click onto sites if the banner ad for the site references the "top," "best," or "most" of anything advertised. We are told every day of our lives that if we have the top, best, or most of anything, we will be happy. And implicitly, we are told that if we don't have the top, best, or most of something, we risk being unhappy.

A lot of this is due to our biology. As a species, we have a very strong animal instinct to survive. This instinct lends itself to competition for scarce resources, whether mates, food, or earthly glory. However, one of the most wonderful things about being human is that we can be happy without competing for these things, because using our human ingenuity, and out of the exercise of prudence, we can figure out how to get what we need to be happy in another way.

THE REAL WAY TO
GET WEALTHY

When you think about it, you realize that there are only four ways to get the things you want: 1) you can steal them; 2) you can gamble and hope to win them; 3) someone can give them to you; or 4) you can trade something else of value in order to get them. These are the only four ways to get the things you want.

It should be obvious that two of these ways are unacceptable: stealing and gambling. Not only are they morally wrong, they are stupid. Even if you were able to pull it off—that is, even if you figured out how to steal or gamble without getting caught or losing everything you had—you would always be at risk for getting caught or losing everything. Neither of these ways is a good method for getting wealthy.

So that brings us to the two other methods: having something given to you, or trading something of value for something you want.

Having things given to you is a blessing of life—

more about that later. For now, let's focus on trading something of value for something you want.

And this is the "real" way you get wealthy: not by competing, but by delivering value to others.

I want to emphasize a particular point: If you want others to give you things of value, ALWAYS seek to create value for them. Every day of your life, seek ways to bring value to others.

When you create value for others, you will receive value in return. It is a law of the universe.

Oddly enough, it is actually easier to figure out what others value and provide that than it is to figure out what we ourselves ought to value. Figuring out what we should value is half the battle of becoming wealthy. We're going to dive into this, but first let's look at the true nature of what wealth really is.

THE TRUE NATURE
OF WEALTH

As we explore the true nature of wealth, let's ask some more "why" questions.

Why would we want to be happy?

Why do we want to get ahead?

Why do we want to succeed?

For what do we hunger?

The answers are really not very hard. In the end, everyone, everywhere, in every place, at every time, wants to be happy. We want to be wealthy, and we want to get ahead, and we want to succeed because we want to be happy. Happiness is that for which we hunger.

I want everyone who is reading this book to be happy, and in fact, being happy is connected to being wealthy. But I want us to think clearly about what that means. I want us to think systematically about wealth, because if we do that, we have a better chance of actually becoming wealthy.

So let's think about wealth. Are you as wealthy as Bill Gates, the founder of Microsoft? Or Mark Zuckerberg, the founder of Facebook? Or the Google guys?

If your answer is no, I want you to think about why you give that answer. I assume it is because you measure your "wealth" in terms of material things. That is Marxism. Karl Marx felt that the only things in life that mattered were material things.

I didn't ask whether you had more money than those rich business titans. I asked whether you were as wealthy as they are. As soon as we measure our "wealth" as a function of material goods, we are thinking like Marxists.

So first we need to understand the true nature of wealth. In fact, we need to develop a philosophy of wealth—*philosophy* coming from the two Greek words for "love" and "wisdom." If we want to be wealthy, we should love the wisdom that teaches us about wealth.

In a way, wealth and sexuality are very similar. Our society is deathly afraid of honest, clear-eyed discussions about either of these topics. The topics are so powerful that we are afraid of an honest dialogue. And because we don't have that honest dialogue, our society jumps in with a dishonest dialogue.

The dishonest dialogue ignores the true blessings of wealth and sexuality, instead focusing on those aspects that are sensational. If we stay focused only on that which is sensational, we will never discover the true wonder of either sex or wealth.

The word *wealth* itself comes from the Middle English word *weal*, meaning "well-being." **Simply put, our wealth is a function of our well-being.** Unfortunately, well-being is hard to quantify, so we use a very very inaccurate shortcut. We instead define wealth as material goods.

But to really understand wealth, we are going to have to think very hard. Because it is hard, let's go step-by-step. Maybe, before defining wealth, we could identify some folks who are wealthy.

Who is really wealthy? Bill Gates, or his children, or his grandchildren?

What do we mean by the term "net worth?" Who is "worth more," me or my two-year-old grandson? I would give up my life to save his, so I think he is "worth more," but he is just two years old, and he has ZERO money. Whose net worth is greater?

King Louis XIV, who built the mind-boggling palace in Versailles, did not have air-conditioning.

Was he wealthier than me? He did not have modern grocery stores, where he could purchase fresh food throughout the year from around the world. Did he have greater wealth—greater well-being?

Is a child who stands to inherit a billion dollars—but is an orphan who never knew either parent—wealthy? What about the children whose parents are going through a divorce? I experienced my own parents' divorce—fortunately when I was older rather than when I was younger. No one in a family going through divorce is wealthy.

Many American scholars have written on the plague of divorce, illegitimacy, and the breakdown of the family. Is the breakdown of our families the sign of what we would call a wealthy society?

The reality is that wealth cannot merely be measured by a country's GDP, and it is not just composed of material things. There is indeed material wealth, but even more important is our emotional wealth, our physical well-being, and our spiritual wealth.

Let's hit the "pause" button for a moment. I realize that what I have just said may sound like a way to rationalize the fact that some folks don't have money; it may sound like I'm implying they ought to be happy anyway. But that's not what I'm talking about.

I discovered these observations about wealth while I was wearing my "money-making hat" in my investment business. In the next chapter I want to take you through a bit of financial analysis in order to demonstrate to you that my study of the world's material wealth helped me to understand the components of true wealth for all of us. You see, I discovered the most important ingredient of wealth when I studied how wealth was lost.

How Does Wealth Disappear?

Let's look again at what happened during the Great Global Credit Crisis of 2008–09. That period is truly a great laboratory of human and social behavior. Let's think about how global wealth was lost during that time.

I remember being struck by an estimate from the US Treasury Department stating that during the crisis, the United States had lost $17 trillion, and the estimate for the amount of wealth that had been lost in the world was $50 trillion! Wow! That is a whole lot of loss!

Where did all that money go? That was the question I started asking myself. I knew that when the Treasury Department said that $50 trillion had been lost, they did not mean that it had been misplaced, such as when someone loses his keys, or a sock. They meant that our collective global assessment of our global wealth had declined immensely.

The market capitalization of a company is the total amount of money the company is worth in the eyes of its stockholders. It is computed by taking all the shares of the company's stock and multiplying that number by the price per share. During the crisis, a company like General Electric, which has been around for over 100 years, lost more than two-thirds of its market capitalization. In other words, the stockholders felt it had lost two thirds of its value within a year or two. Why?

I reasoned that if we could figure out how that much wealth is "lost," we could also get an idea of how it can be "found."

About that time, I ran across a market report from PIMCO. PIMCO is the largest money manager in the world—they manage over $1 trillion dollars. This is what the report said (boldface added):

Whether evolution or revolution it is important to recognize that the aftermath of an economic and investment bubble transitioning from levering to de-levering, globalization to de-globalization and lax regulation to reregulation leads to an across-the-board rise in risk premiums, higher volatility and therefore *lower asset prices for a majority of asset classes.* [I know some of this sounds like gobbledygook, but keep going.] The journey to a new stasis is a destructive one insofar as it affects previously assumed wealth. Rough estimates suggest that as much as 40% of global wealth has been destroyed since the beginning of this de-levering process. In essence, asset prices, which are really only the discounted **future value** of wealth creation, go down— not only because that wealth creation slows down but because it becomes **more uncertain.** In such an environment, equity interests in the form of stocks, real estate or . . . bonds become **re-rated.**

Interests become "re-rated"? What does that mean? And 40 percent of global wealth was *destroyed?* How does *that* happen?

THE FIRST ESSENTIAL INGREDIENT OF WEALTH IS HOPE

One of the critical points I want to make here, as someone who lives and breathes every day in the world of finance, is that material wealth is inherently a function of hope. Hope is an expectation of the future, and wealth (our well-being), while lived in the present, is predominantly governed by our expectations for the future.

This is how it works in the real world of financial investments. Every share of stock in a publicly-traded company has a ratio known as a "P/E" ratio. The "P/E" stands for "Price to Earnings." The price that people will pay for a share of stock in a business is based on what they think the business will earn in the future. If they think the business is only going to make money for another two years, they would not pay more than about 2 times the earnings of the company, and the share price of the stock would have a P/E of approximately 2. If they think the business is going to make money for a long time, and that the amount of money the business might make each year will grow, they may pay a price per share that would result in a P/E of 50.

What happened during the Great Global Credit Crisis of 2008–09 was that assets like stocks got "re-rated." In other words, the hope that everyone had for the future was greatly diminished, and so companies that were selling for a P/E of 40 now sold for a P/E of 10, and companies that were selling for a P/E of 15 went down to a P/E of 5. They were re-rated.

You see, in the end, even things in the financial world, such as stocks and bonds, are inevitably a reflection of things that are not material, such as hope.

And that's why we have to adopt a different definition of wealth, because the one focused merely on that which is material ends up being woefully insufficient. I would like to suggest this definition of wealth:

> Wealth is a measure of our well-being, **most accurately** measured in the quality of our human capital and relationships, and the **hope and expectations** of those relationships.

Is Bill Gates wealthy? What if I told you he just found out he has one day to live? Is he still wealthy? How much do you think he would pay for ten more years? $50 billion? By the way, if he dies tomorrow, he will be, by the definition of the world, WORTHLESS—i.e., worth nothing! Isn't that amazing? And his business empire will decline in value, because our hope in the future growth of that empire will have declined. That value didn't go anywhere—it just vanished. That wealth is gone. **Wealth can be created out of thin air when hope increases, and it can vanish into thin air when hope is diminished.**

Why does this seem hard to accept? Well, we have all become materialists. Because we have physical bodies made of matter, we forget that we are more than just material.

A few years ago, in an audience with civic authorities, Pope Benedict XVI was addressing the economic crisis. He said that the first step toward creating a wealthier society is to "rediscover relationships as *the* constituent element of our lives." How many of us believe that relationships are *the* constituent element of our lives? In other words, how many of us believe that relationships are the *most important element* in terms of what constitutes our lives?

Think about the Great Global Credit Crisis. Think about the root of the word *credit*. The root of that word is *credo*, meaning "to believe." When I extend credit to someone, I am expressing a belief in them. My extension of credit is evidence of a human relationship. If I do not have *hope* in the other person, if I do not have a good expectation for the future, the relationship will not prosper.

It is the same with a marriage—we begin with hopeful expectations for the future of the relationship. But when the hope dries up, there is a vicious cycle of relationship dysfunction. And that is why so many people don't feel wealthy—it is a comment on lost hope in the future! In particular, our Western culture has lost hope in the family.

And so we find ourselves in a situation in which our wealth is diminishing because our relationships are diminishing, because our hope is diminishing. And if we are to repair our wealth, and indeed grow our wealth, we must be aware of the transgressions we have committed against hope; we must look into any disorder we have created within our human relationships.

As a businessman I can tell you, with certainty, that when hope disappears, there will be no fruitful investment, and when hope is alive, the world prospers with human ingenuity. Google sells at a P/E of 35. In other words, the company is valued at 35 times the amount of money it will make this year. At the end of 2016, it was worth over half a trillion dollars. Why does something sell for a P/E of 35? Because of the expectations for the future. If legislation outlawed their search techniques, what would happen to the P/E multiple? It would plummet. It would go to 5, and the value of the company would go down more than 80 percent. The market capitalization of Google's stock is a function of hope in the future—destroy the hope, destroy the wealth. Enhance the hope, enhance the wealth.

Hope is the first essential ingredient of all true wealth.

THE SECOND ESSENTIAL INGREDIENT OF WEALTH IS HUMAN RELATIONSHIPS

So far we've looked at reality, we have looked at the nature of wealth, and we have explored the first component of wealth: hope. We will conclude by examining how our human relationships make us wealthy.

Does reducing wealth to a combination of hope and human relationships sound too easy? Well, in a way, it is easy, in that it is simple. But in reality, it is not easy. Simple does not mean easy. The process of dunking a basketball is actually fairly simple, but I have never been able to do it, other than on an eight-foot rim!

No, hope is not an easy virtue to exercise, and human relationships are never, ever easy. But if we want to be wealthy, we have to be willing to look at reality, and see things as they really are. What destroys well-being (wealth) and what creates it?

I told you at the beginning of this book that I wanted to change how you look at the world.

First, you have to get comfortable with reality.

Second, you have to be careful about the games in which you compete, and not view competition as the route to happiness.

Third, you have to understand the true sources of wealth.

And fourth, you have to figure out how to get those real sources of wealth. So let's dive into that now. Remember the definition of wealth: "Wealth is a measure of our well-being, **most accurately** measured in the quality of our human capital and relationships, and the **hope and expectations** of those relationships."

Do you want to be happy, or do you want to win?

I'll let you in on a secret—the secret of success! And the reason I'm sharing it with you is that I want you to be happy. I desperately want for you to be happy. You may say, "How can you want me to be happy—you don't even know me." But think about it: When you are watching your favorite football team, you root for the running back to cross the goal line and score even if you do not personally know him. Why? Because he is on your team! You have a stake in your team, and you want your team to do well. Well, I have a stake in you. You are a member of my team. And you were *made* to be happy.

As we go about our daily lives in the midst of the world, it is important that we properly understand what it means to be happy. Because the world we live in fills us with misguided notions of what can make us happy. Unfortunately, when the world says, "Hey, as long as it makes you happy," what is really meant is "Hey, as long as you *feel* OK about it right now, it is OK." But we all know that a temporary feeling doesn't necessarily lead to happiness.

So what does truly make you happy? I want you to stop reading for just a moment, close your eyes, and think about someone you love, or someone who loves you. Does that make you happy? It does me. Do you know why? The answer to that question is actually the secret to happiness . . . and the secret to being wealthy.

Just as we were not made to be unhappy, we were not made to be alone. It is hard to be happy when you are lonely. We are not complete when we are alone; instead, we crave being whole. If you have bad eyes, like me, and you wake up in the morning, the first things you crave are your eyeglasses or your contacts.

We want our vision to be whole, to be complete, and when we can't see, it frustrates us.

Well, that's how our hearts are. We are restless until we feel complete.

We desire to be whole, and when we are whole, we can be happy. The purpose of the next stage of your life is for you to become a more complete person. Did you ever see the movie *Secretariat*, about perhaps the greatest racehorse of all time? Toward the end, as he runs down the homestretch in his final race, going faster and faster, you get chills watching him. Do you know why you get chills? Because you are seeing a creature do exactly what it was intended to do—fulfilling its potential.

So what will help you fulfill *your* potential, making you whole, and thereby wealthy?

There is a word that unlocks the secret to this wholeness about which I am speaking. That word is *communion*. Communion is what we really want in our relationships. We want communion with each other. We want *common union* with each other. We crave communion, and in fact, we cannot live without it.

When we gather together with others for a common purpose, we have a common union; we become a communion. We have communion, and since it is a good purpose that we have in common, it is a communion that makes us happy.

There are large communions, such as a crowd gathered for a football game. Why is it so much more fun to go to a game than to watch it on TV? It is the *communion* we get to share with all the other fans who have gathered with us. Think of the feeling we get when we share such an experience with 90,000 other people.

In our relationships we all *need* communion so badly, we crave it so badly, so desperately, that we will feverishly seek to obtain it. We need it to survive, and we will do anything to get it.

And so here is the secret of life! **In fact, if you do what I am about to tell you, I guarantee that you WILL be wealthy.**

The secret of life is to seek and enter into true communion with others, and avoid false and hollow communion. If you do that you *will* be wealthy and happy!

I am fifty-four years old. I have had a fair amount of material success, I have had my share of meeting Hollywood stars, Wall Street moguls, presidents, and even popes, and none of that matters compared to my relationships. Every bit of true communion I have had has brought me fulfillment, and every bit of false communion I have had has brought me grief.

You may say, "OK, but how do I know which is true and which is false?" Well, the essence is this: True communion is communion that has a good and true purpose—a common union with the Truth. And false communion is a common union with that which is not the Truth. A one-night stand, for example, is a false communion.

And here's what's interesting with relationships: You *will* have one or the other. You cannot avoid communion—it would be like avoiding breathing. You will form attachments, because nature abhors a vacuum, and you must have communion to survive. And so you will either have true communion or false communion. And by the way, if you have enough true communion, you can crowd out the false communion.

You can also have communion with people who have provided immortal good communion with others. When you listen to the music of Beethoven, you have communion with him. And when you read good authors, you have good communion, whether with Dostoevsky, Shakespeare, Aristotle, or Flannery O'Connor.

That's how you get wealthy—you establish communion with good people.

Why Good Communion Works

There are a few very logical reasons why establishing communion with good people will make you wealthy. We've said that "wealth is a measure of our well-being, **most accurately** measured in the quality of our human capital and relationships, and the **hope and expectations** of those relationships." If this is true, then we must cultivate hope and human relationships above all else.

First, no one is truly wealthy without communion with others.

Second, while hope is a necessary component for wealth, the most sure-fire way of increasing your hope is actually to have good communion with good people.

Third, when you have good communion with good people, you will naturally want to provide value to them. And when you provide value to others, you will receive value yourself. The whole idea is to have an abundance of that which you value.

Fourth, if you establish communion with good people, it will teach you to be unselfish. To create wealth, you must be unselfish. To be happily married, you must be unselfish. To be a good parent, you must be unselfish. To be a good friend, you must be unselfish.

Fifth, if you truly learn how to be unselfish, you will become heroic. I don't mean you'll be like Superman or Wonder Woman; instead you will be heroic for others. Think of the person you most respect—you can become that for someone else, and that too is a source of wealth. Not for the ego involved, but for the gift you give.

GOING FORWARD

You may not think you have any wealth at all, but by now, you should know that wealth is your well-being, so you do have some. But I want you to get more! I want you to become really wealthy. Therefore, my challenge to you is to reassess the true nature of your wealth, of your well-being. Do you have a strategy to enhance your well-being? Or do you have a strategy that *unintentionally* destroys that well-being?

As you finish this book, your first task is to continually seek wisdom in life. Wisdom is not the same as knowledge; wisdom comes from the understanding of reality we discussed at the beginning—the ability to see things as they really are, without delusion, and then have the courage to take the right action in light of that reality.

If you continually seek wisdom, you will then begin to eliminate the things that destroy your wealth: bad habits, bad values, bad competitions, and bad relationships.

Your second task is to start looking for good people with whom you can have good communion.

Your third task is to seek ways daily to provide value to others, rather than to compete with them.

Your fourth task is to be hopeful. And the best way to do this is to have good communion with others.

Do you know why old people in nursing homes love to have visitors, but truly light up when they see a child? It's because a child represents hope in the future! Even if they only have a week, or a month, or an hour to live, the child increases their wealth! That is what hope can do.

I faced something similar four years ago when my daughter got married. What would have taken me away from that wedding? How much money? It was the best night of my life! I have learned that the greatest source of happiness is seeing someone you love experience joy. And wedding nights fill us all with great hope—for the happiness that we wish for the future. That night, I truly believe I was the wealthiest man on the planet!

That is, until my new grandson came along . . . he fills me with so much hope, that now I *know* I am the wealthiest man on the planet.

What about you? I can't let this opportunity go by

without asking you: Are you looking to get married? Why wouldn't you be? You can postpone it, but there is a risk to postponement. You don't want to be competing for sex and friendship and companionship and love and care for the next twenty-five years. Instead, find someone with whom you can have abundance as soon as possible. Abundance, not scarcity, is the hallmark of wealth. In my home, we don't compete for love—we have an abundance of it! I don't want to compete for it! Find someone with whom you can share a lifetime of abundance.

Ask yourself, "Am I actively working on the skills I need to be happily married? Do I even know what those skills are? If not, why not?"

Because of my line of work, I have run across a bunch of billionaires. Yes, billion, with a B. I am not a billionaire, but I know a lot of them. I was thinking about it the other day, and I realized that some of them are happy, but many of them are not. And then I realized that for those who were happy, the common denominator is not that they were billionaires, because many of the billionaires were actually unhappy. The common denominator for the ones who are happy is that they are happily married. The billionaires who are not happily married have a much harder time being happy.

In feudal times, material wealth was represented by land. Today we may see it represented by businesses or the earning potential in a career. But is land, or a business, or a career truly the constituent element of wealth? Or are the constituent elements, the most fundamental elements of our wealth, the relationships we have and the hope we have for the future?

And if we believe that the answer is relationships and hope, are we living as if that were true? Are you looking for good relationships, particularly with a spouse, and are you preparing yourself to be a good spouse? Are you planning to have children? Are you developing virtue in yourself? Are you developing the virtue of hope and trying to practice it every day? Are you learning to bring value to others?

This book is an exercise in hope—my hope for your future wealth. I hope it has also brought value to your life.